The Bluebonnet Sutras

The Bluebonnet Sutras

Laurence Musgrove

LITERARY PRESS
LAMAR UNIVERSITY

ISBN: 978-1-942956-72-3
Library of Congress Control Number: 9781942956723

Artwork by Myra Musgrove
Editor: Lillian Hill
Cover Photo: Tim Geers

Lamar University Literary Press
Beaumont, Texas

For
Marie-Clare

Recent Poetry from Lamar University Literary Press

Bobby Aldridge, *An Affair of the Stilled Heart*
Walter Bargen, *My Other Mother's Red Mercedes*
Julie Chappell, *Mad Habits of a Life*
Stan Crawford, *Resisting Gravity*
Chip Dameron, *Waiting for an Etcher*
Glover Davis, *My Cap of Darkness*
William Virgil Davis, *The Bones Poems*
Jeffrey DeLotto, *Voices Writ in Sand*
Chris Ellery, *Elder Tree*
Alan Gann, *That's Entertainment*
Larry Griffin, *Cedar Plums*
Michelle Hartman, *Irony and Irrelevance*
Katherine Hoerth, *Goddess Wears Cowboy Boots*
Michael Jennings, *Crossings: A Record of Travel*
Gretchen Johnson, *A Trip Through Downer, Minnesota*
Ulf Kirchdorfer, *Chewing Green Leaves*
Jim McGarrah, *A Balancing Act*
J. Pittman McGehee, *Nod of Knowing*
Laurence Musgrove, *One Kind of Recording*
Godspower Oboido, *Wandering Feet on Pebbled Shores*
Carol Coffee Reposa, *Underground Musicians*
Jan Seale, *The Parkinson Poems*
Steven Schroeder, *the moon, not the finger, pointing*
Glen Sorestad, *Hazards of Eden*
Vincent Spina, *The Sumptuous Hills of Gulfport*
W.K. Stratton, *Ranchero Ford/Dying in Red Dirt Country*
Wally Swist, *Invocation*
Loretta Diane Walker, *Desert Light*
Dan Williams, *Past Purgatory, a Distant Paradise*
Jonas Zdanys, *Three White Horses*

For information on these and other Lamar University Literary Press books go to www.Lamar.edu/literarypress.

Acknowledgments

I would also like to express my gratitude to the numerous journals and anthologies that originally published many of these poems:

Inside Higher Ed
Moment
San Antonio Express-News
Red River Review
Elephant Journal

CONTENTS

V: Harmony of Birds

VI: Our Minds

VII: Encourage

VIII: Into Flight

IX: Listen Again

I: Horizon

Unfinished Sutra

When I met the Buddha
On the road, I was worried
He would see the litter
Of my wasted life behind me.

All I wanted was for him
To whisper courage
Into my exhausted heart
So I could make it to tomorrow.

"I was once afraid like you,"
He said, "until I learned
Time is no sand in the glass
And not this road we share.

"Time is not a tree
With leaves upon the ground
Or even the monsoon
Ravaging the hungry valley.

"Time is not a dying fire
Or the moon chasing
The sun around the sky.
Time is not a wheel.

"Time is not a bell.
Not a ringing bowl.
Time is not a shadow
Underneath a cloud.

"Time is not a memory.
Time is not a dream.
Time is not your children.
Not your father's coat.

"Time was never born.
Time can never die.
Time has no master.
Time cannot hide."

As I walked with the Buddha,
Darkness followed close behind us.
But on the long road before us,
The sun melted and froze on the horizon.

II: To Sit There

Desire Sutra

When I was standing
Outside the Buddha's
Hut as he discussed
The nature of desire
With his advanced
Students, I heard one
Of the elders ask him
If the ultimate goal
Was to heal suffering
By extinguishing desire.
And the Buddha told
Him his question was
A very excellent one
And answered smiling,

"Because desire is eternal,
It can only be redirected
Away from the darkness
Of our common suffering
And toward the light
Of self-understanding.
In this way, we can know
The shine of ongoing
Consciousness that
Awakens our conscience
And courageous compassion."

And the silence of the hut
Was easily consumed by
The song of autumn
In the crisp leaves
Of the forest overhead.

Ego Sutra

I was telling the Buddha
How much I was looking
Forward to the weekend
After a fairly stressful
Couple of days at school.

"I've had to deal with some
 Inflated egos, and I've also
 Gotten behind in my grading."

He said, "The ego is one
Of my favorite topics.
Many believe the ego is a sign
Of power and authority
Captured through experience.
However, the ego on display
Is like a loud braggart
Hiding his fear and ignorance
With threats and blame.
In truth, as the ego matures,
It actually becomes smaller
And quieter because it learns
Authority can only be located
In the respect and kindness
We give away freely to others,
Like to those students whose
Papers you'll soon be grading."

Awake Sutra

I showed the Buddha the exercise
I planned for my students in making
An image of the meditating Buddha
By stacking three small balls of paper.
I then asked him why he thought
Most images of the Buddha depicted
His face with closed and smiling eyes.

"There are many ways to be awakened
 Into mindfulness," he said.
"We can choose to wake ourselves
 Out of the slumber of distraction,
 Or we can be startled awake because
 We had not prepared for the unexpected.
 Meditation helps us see what deserves
 Our attention and what does not.
 Then, we can select what we believe
 Deserves our most focused attention.
 This practice, of course, never ends,
 But with each attempt our focus arrives
 More quickly and more deeply
 As we strengthen our appreciation
 Of what deserves our attention.
 And the eyes always reflect this joy."

Retreat Sutra

Our trip to the Zen retreat center
In Sante Fe was about a month away,
And I told the Buddha how much
I was looking forward to the chance
To have more time and fewer distractions
As I searched for a greater understanding
Of my role in improving society.

He said, "Retreats clearly provide
A setting for more effective meditation
And the strengthening of the habits
Of wakefulness and compassion.
But in the long run, they're just retreats.
The real challenge is coming home to
The daily tests of your mind and heart
With the courage necessary to embrace
The world unfolding in front of you."

Trout Sutra

I was meditating on *shenpa* today
Because of how often I am hooked
Into the habits of fearful response
When I encounter those people
And daily responsibilities
That intensify my path of suffering.
I was telling the Buddha how I was
Looking for some helpful teaching
Or image that would awaken me
To these automatic failures.

"The hook," said the Buddha,
"May be a worn metaphor to some,
 But consider the skill of the catch
 And the joy of the release the angler
 Must feel in cradling the trout
 And then freeing it to swim away.
 Every hook will be barbless when
 You can catch yourself being caught."

23

Slow and Strong Sutra

When I joked with the Buddha,
I said, "It's like you have a
PhD in Time Management."

He said, "What you say is really
Funny to me, but only partly true.
There is also the matter of speed.
When we desire to gain time,
We slow ourselves down long enough
To understand how to strengthen our lives
In the service of strengthening others."

"Wow," I said. "That might take a long time for me."

"Like I said," he said, "slowing down and strengthening
Are matters of desire,
Not time."

Throne Sutra

This morning in sitting practice,
Given my tendency to slouch,
I focused on straightening my back.

I pictured myself on a throne,
A calm king of my bodily realm.
And I realized how fortunate I was
To have had a childhood free of
Fear and anger that I know often
Rule other families, a father or mother
Who suffer in sadness or desertion
Or pain who pull others down
As they drown in a dark flood
Of tears deepening around them.

So I returned my attention to my breath
And began to feel a bright compassion
Sitting high on the throne of my mind.

Then I asked His Royal Prince Gautama,
"What do you recall about your father
And how he sat upon his throne?"

The Buddha replied with his smile,
"My father was a very kind man,
A generous ruler of his kingdom.
And my mother was a loving queen.
They made it possible for me to see
It was my birthright to show others
How to achieve their royalty, too.
That's why I had to leave the palace
After seeing the suffering outside.
Each of our lives is a kingdom.

"Each of our minds is a throne.
Who do we want to sit there?"

III: Others

CROSBY, STILLS & NASH

Forgiving Sutra

While the Buddha was
In a retreat of unknown
Length in the South,
We were talking about
The pull of the past
And wondering what
He would say about
How much we both
Fiercely ignore history
While also wishing
We could return to
A dream time that
Never existed.

Then we decided what
He'd say about the past
Is that the people there
Need all the courage
We can create among us,
Because if we are ever
Going to take control
Of our minds at last,
We will have to forgive
The past that shaped us.

Story Sutra

When I returned to my office after class,
The Buddha was waiting to see if I wanted
To go grab a coffee at the new Starbucks.
I told him that I had just finished teaching
One of my favorite Tobias Wolff stories
"Hunters in the Snow," and he told me,

"You are fortunate to have the job you do.
Reading fiction reminds us of the value
Of developing the narrative consciousness
Necessary to reflect on how we are written
By others and how we also write ourselves.
Students must come to see themselves
As the author-hero of their own stories,
Learning how to overcome the obstacles
They encounter and more often those
They unknowingly put in their own way.
In the case of this story, one I also admire,
We learn we are all in danger of being idiots,
Slaves to fear and craving and ignorance."

At Ease Sutra

for Army Cadet Lee

After receiving an email from a university
Colleague who thanked me for supporting
His son's application to West Point,
I showed the Buddha the attached photos
And videos my friend took at Reception Day,
With more than 1200 cadets parading into
The Plain at the Academy as they prepared
To begin their first six weeks of basic training.

"I like watching these young men and women
 Marching in unison and standing at attention,"
The Buddha said, "and when they are told
 To stand at ease, you know that they are still
Very much at attention, their shoulders back
And strong, their eyes still clear and ready.
This kind of at ease attention is what we all
Hope for ourselves, a calm, sharp mind
In constant defense of what we love most."

Clear Sutra
for Shastri Linda M.

After arriving home from the weekend retreat
At the Shambhala Center in San Antonio, I told
The Buddha how happy I was to encounter new
Practices in walking meditation, contemplation,
And for the first time feel confident sitting
On the cushion, "At last, I was able to receive
Personal, expert, and corrective instruction."

"I can already see," he said, "a new integrity
 In your posture. The value of an experienced
 Teacher is essential to improving your practice.
 When we are trained out of our confusion,
 The dark sediment of self-doubt falls away,
 And in its place, the joy of clear intention."

Privilege Sutra

I was telling the Buddha
About a new friend of mine,
An inmate serving 42 years,
Who sent me a letter
Seeking help with his poetry.

I said, "We've been writing
Each other for a year now,
And his poetry keeps getting
Better and better all the time.
I admire his confidence and hope."

He said, "The world we are born into
Will seem natural to us, good or bad.
We can only know what's ours to know.
So when we struggle for a different world,
It will seem unnatural, and thus, doubly hard."

Impatience Sutra

I was whining to the Buddha
About my lack of mindfulness
Because I was distracting myself
With hope for a better life ahead.

"Your impatience with the present
About a future you desire
Is the only chance the future has
To trap you in the past.

"Why waste the only time you have
On a time you may not get?"

Practice Sutra

The checkout line at the HEB
Was longer than usual today,
So I turned to the Buddha
And said, "It looks like we have
Some time for discussion now,
So let me ask you to clarify
What you were saying earlier
About the practices that have
Been passed down and those
That have not been transmitted."

And the Buddha smiled and said,
"The focus from the beginning
 Was on recording the practices
 That created beneficial capacities
 In fearlessness and compassion
 So we could then transmit that
 Mental discipline to others in need.
 And because the general practice
 Is designed to generate specific
 And unique benefits for each of us,
 It would have been impossible to
 Record and then transmit every
 Insight gained and practiced.
 This is the universal wisdom
 Of our teaching: the *dharma*
 Offers you a well-worn path
 To a place only you will see."

Spring Sutra

I was pulling weeds
This morning while
It was still pleasant
And cool in the shade,
And I got a call from
The Buddha checking
In on me because
Of our long talk
Last night about
All I had planned
To catch up on this
Week but hadn't
Exactly gotten to.

"The work you are
 Doing outside will
 Be good for you.
 When we add
 Ourselves to nature
 We receive a lesson
 And enjoy spring's
 Confidence in us
 And the world."

Spare Room Sutra

When the Buddha
Was visiting from
Out of town,
We put him up
In the spare bedroom.
And after dinner
He and I began to
List for each other
Our favorite albums
From our time
Together in college,
Marveling at the
Surge of creativity
That seems to come
During periods of
Conflict and change.

And he said to me
How sad his heart
Became when he
Thought about
How much light,
Power, and joy
Is available
To each of us,
And how easily
They are wasted
In wrong feelings
About ourselves
And others.

IV: In His Hand

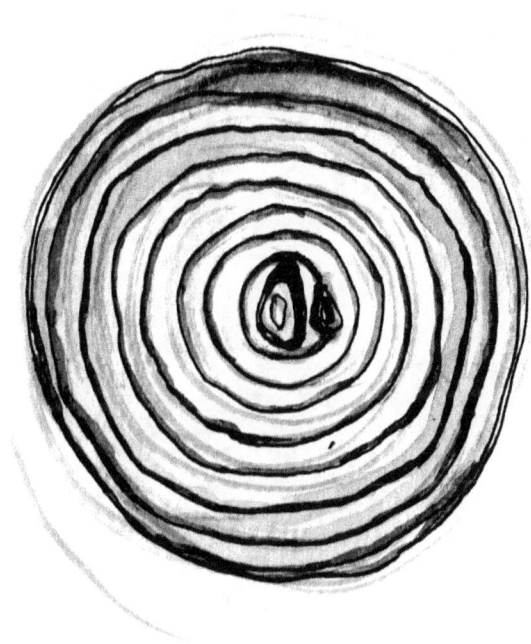

Sin Sutra

As the Buddha walked slowly upon the high path
Next to the stream running below the cold mountain,
I quietly asked his attendants for permission to approach
So I could ask our teacher about the nature of sin and desire.

He said, "The sinful ride the unbridled horse of desire.
But who opened the gate so the horse could run away?
And who reached up and removed the bridle?
These are very important questions that should be asked.

"Many prefer the much easier path and blame the sinner
Rather than look for the one who left the gate open.
We should also ask who among us removed the bridle.
The sinner is only a student of the desire the world has made.

"We walk a much more difficult path in our understanding
Of the nature of desire and sin because we have decided
To mend the suffering of our wounded hearts and minds
By rejecting the book of desire which is written by the world.

"Instead, we strive to be the stone tossed into the stream
Creating a constant and infinite circle of forgiveness.
Our teachings must also show how to close the open gate.
They must teach us how to reach up and secure the bridle.

"To be clear, sin is not a cause but an effect of desire.
We must learn that sin does not originate in the sinful
But in the sin of those who profit from our desire and sin.
We desire for students of the world a different school."

Syllabus Sutra

I was explaining to the Buddha
How I was thinking about the focus
And design of the composition course
I would be teaching this coming fall.
I said, "I'm thinking about the combined
Themes of self-discovery and service."

He said, "I appreciate that approach.
Each of us has the obligation
To find and follow the self
We inherited from our ancestors.
The search to end our suffering
Will be satisfied more quickly
Once we understand this goal
And sharpen our attention, but
Let's not stand in each other's way
Of finding the way that is ours.
We should belong to each other
In our longing to be ourselves."

Literature Sutra
for Brian Turner

I was telling the Buddha about
The writers conference last week
And how much I enjoyed hearing
The poems and stories of others.
I asked him what he thought
Literature's contribution might be
To creating an enlightened society.

"We all have and then lose ideas.
 Some of us don't have any idea
 We are having and losing them.
 Some of us are very aware
 We are beginning to forget things.
 And some feel under constant
 Attack by the ideas of others.
 Still others of us have learned
 In our meditation practice,
 The importance of holding
 On to ideas as long as we can.
 We come to understand that
 The longer we can hold on
 The better we will be at
 Knowing when to let that idea go.
 Or we may decide it's a keeper
 And grasp it as tight as we can.
 Reading and writing not only
 Help us hold on to our ideas
 But provide us with reports
 On how the having, the holding,
 The losing, and the letting go
 Happened to those before us."

Training Sutra

It was my wife's idea
To attend the 10-day
Vipassana meditation
Retreats this summer.
I told the Buddha
I planned to go in May
And she in August.

I said, "When I realized
I wouldn't be allowed
To bring any books
Or writing materials,
I understood just how
Dependent I'd become
On their company.
I wonder how I will
Manage without them."

He said, "The practices
You will learn require
All of your attention.
The demands are high.
You are training your mind
To listen to your body
So it can prepare your heart
For a future you can't imagine."

Listen Sutra

I told the Buddha I was
Beginning to hear his voice
In my head more often.

I said, "If I told anybody
I was hearing voices,
They'd think I was crazy."

He said, "If the only voice
You listened to was your own,
You'd be crazy, too."

Eye Sutra

During my midday walk with the Buddha,
I felt at ease enough to tell him of my trouble
In contemplation and how my mind
Was constantly drifting into feelings of regret
And worry for all the troubles of tomorrow.

The Buddha turned to me on the road
And pointed to his eyes, saying
"The problem is primarily a visual confusion."
He then lowered himself onto his heels,
And began to draw in the dirt between us.

"Let us say this small dot I've made with my finger
Represents your understanding of the present.
And this line I draw to your right is your future worry.
And this line I draw to your left is your past regret.
But these are false images and must be erased.

"Given that this moment is all we can really have,
The more accurate depiction of the present is
This round image of the eye, open and kind.
Raise your eyes from the ground and see the horizon.
The sun and moon chase each other in the sky.

"The tear on your check is round, and so is the eye.
These beggar bowls are round, as are the ripples
In the river from the rain when it falls.
The present can be as infinite as the dome of heaven,
Where the mind and heart can embrace at last."

Canoe Sutra

for Andrew Geyer

The Buddha told me that since I had
So many questions, it would be best
If I took a turn in the front of the canoe.
For a good part of our morning together,
The water was exceedingly calm and wide,
So I asked him how he lived on the other
Side of his enlightenment, wondering
What more there was to learn after
Attaining such exalted consciousness.

He said that our minds have a thirst
Larger than any river we paddle down,
"When Milton began to lose the light
 And Beethoven saw silence coming from
 The strings, they found a way to hear
 Without hearing and to see without sight."

Onion Sutra

I was standing in the kitchen
Preparing the evening meal
While at the table, the Buddha
Sat and checked his email.
I asked him if he could define
Fundamental goodness, a concept
I had struggled with during
My morning sitting practice,
"I wonder if I'm confusing
Selfless acts with a basic trait
We all share, some inherited
Potential for joy and love."

The Buddha smiled and said,
"The light we're born with
Is like a flame that's never
Without fuel, though we soon
Learn to hide it under our fears.
Then we forget it's even there.
Look at the onion you're about
To slice open on the counter.
As the bulb of the onion grows
From its center, it expands
Adding layer upon thin layer,
Covering itself in a hard dry coat
To protect the heart of its flavor.
But the onion is no good to us
Until that dry skin is torn off
And the layers are cut apart.
It's just the same with me and you.
When we hide our basic goodness
In layers of anxiety and aggression,
We cannot see the light within us.

"As with that onion, many tears
Will fall as you reveal the heart
You've waited so long to open."

Broom Sutra

What I like most about working in the yard
Is that it gives me a lot of time to think,
Even though my body isn't all that happy

About the mowing and the trimming part.
I also like that my neighbor the Buddha
Will often come over to talk to me about

The parade of my imagination.
For example, today I was picturing all of
The different ways people use a broom.

There are those who like to push a wide
Brush of a broom all the way down the long
Quiet hallway of the future in front of them.

Also there are those who love the short
Stroke of a broom in the here and now.
In the late hot afternoon, I swept dry

Clippings into small piles along the curb.
Next, I walked around with a bucket
And squatted down to pick up the piles.

Then, crouched as I was, I saw his shadow
Walking toward me over the even grass,
Ice cubes singing in the glass in his hand.

V: Harmony of Birds

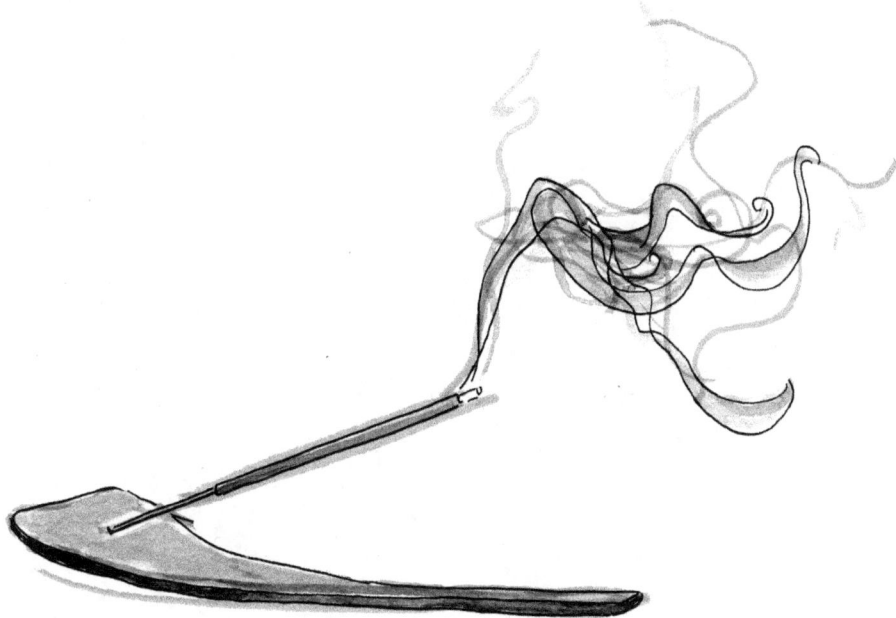

Courage Sutra

We were spending the warm afternoon
With the Buddha in sitting meditation,
And afterward he said, "Let me now
Try to answer the questions you have."

A young woman was first to raise her hand,
"Was there a time when you were fearful?"

"Oh, yes, I was fearful before I knew it.
I once believed I could turn fear on and off,
But it's not like that. Fear is always with us.
That's why we meditate: to find fear.
And as soon as fear knows we see it,
It becomes afraid and runs for cover.
But sooner or later, it always comes back.
Still, we should be thankful for its return.
We can't make our courage without it."

School Sutra

I was at school today responding
To my graduate students' essays
In an online course on reading,
Writing, and teaching poetry.
I told the Buddha how many of
These students had described
Poems as obscure word objects
Owned and operated by schools
Rather than as personally meaningful
And publically significant art forms
Designed to instruct us in empathy,
Mindfulness, and courage. He said,

"Once we accept that learning about
The self is a task with no certain end,
We understand that our education
Cannot be confined by time and place.
It's true that an experienced teacher
Is vital in preparing us to become
Lifelong students of ourselves,
Others, and the world outside,
But these are only initial practices.
Those who have stopped learning
Are asleep in a world that's gone by."

Future Sutra

Last night, the Buddha and I stopped by
The student open mic event on campus.
There were slam poetry readings, karaoke
Sing-alongs, and a large happy audience
Of students lounging on fat sofas.
I told him I often forget how old I am
Compared to my students and hope that
They don't see my age as an obstacle to
Their progress in the world. He said,

"A better future lives in these students
 Here among us, and though we may fear
 The loss of what we hold as timeless,
 Our task should be to teach the traditions
 Of progress that have gotten us this far
 So that they might see the future as a right
 We all share, an inheritance to improve."

Weeping Sutra

On the fifth day
Of the meditation retreat,
And only the second day
Of Vipassana training,
I found myself weeping
How much I missed my teachers.

"A thirst for learning
 Brings tears of insight,"
 The Buddha told me.
"Now think of those
 Who never find these tears,
 Who never benefit from
 The loving-kindness of teachers,
 Who never learn the path
 Out of their suffering.
 Let us weep for them together.
 May they hear and find us."

Brain Sutra

I was telling the Buddha
About the article I had
Read on the benefits of
Meditation as revealed
In new brain research.

And he said, "This is good
News for brain research,
But our practice of mental
Discipline really requires
No scientific justification.
The benefit of frequent
Visits to the mind to focus
And calm one's thinking
Has been demonstrated
By generations of scholars
In many disciplines, but
As I said, good for them."

Open Sutra

After my morning meditation, I asked the Buddha
About the similarities between open-mindedness
And present-mindfulness because I was troubled
By how vulnerable I felt in opening myself up to
Everything that seemed to want to grab ahold of
My attention and lead me outside myself. He said,

"We leave the windows of our minds open so that
The fresh air will ventilate useless ways of thinking,
But it's also possible that a stiff wind will threaten
To topple over what we love and want to keep upright,
And then there is the dust we must keep wiping away
From our minds. So clearly, there will always be work
When we open ourselves, and the always never stops."

Dishes Sutra

After the dinner dishes,
 I asked the Buddha,
"Why is it that we believe
 We have a better chance
 At perfecting the world
 When those before us
 Thought their chances
 Were just as good?"

He said, "The dinner
You prepared tonight was
Particularly satisfying to me
Because there was nothing
Wasteful about its preparation,
Its consumption, or even
The cleaning up afterward,
So you know what I mean
When I say that although
Our excellent meal together
Is ultimately inconsequential
When set against the history
Of human desire and hunger
In the infinite stretch of time,
We should still dedicate
The little time given to us
To the everlasting appetite
Of creating a better world."

Planet Sutra

On Earth Day, the Buddha
Came over for dinner,
And we talked in sadness
About our damaged globe.

He said, "Think of incense
And the ash that falls below.
Desire is also fragrant
But makes too much ash."

Green Sutra

Now that spring was here,
I texted the Buddha
To see if he had time
To come over to see
The roses in our garden
And hear the mourning doves
And mockingbirds
Filling our yard with song.

"Each season," he said,
"Reality beyond experience
Offers itself up to us in
New colors and sounds,
Like the flowers and birds
You want to share with me.
The greenest of seasons
Is the favorite of many
Because we've waited
So long for the sun's return,
And we warm our whistles
To the harmony of birds."

VI: Our Minds

Suffering and Joy Sutra
for Joe

When the Buddha had completed
His discourse before the crowd
Of more than one hundred monks
On the contemplation of suffering,

One of the monks seated near him
Said to the Buddha,

              "Why, Teacher,
is it that we must only contemplate
suffering and not contemplate joy?"

And in response the Buddha smiled
And then bowed his head in silence.

Other monks heard this question
And many nodded in agreement.
"That was a very good question!"

Whispering and quiet debates
Spread quickly through the crowd.

Finally, the Buddha raised his head
And spoke to the curious monk,
"Contemplation is the joy, my friend."

Audition Sutra

I was telling the Buddha
How my studies in literature
Once again reminded me
Of the core metaphor in the story:
Whether the character is
Climbing out of a well
Or scaling a mountain,
All plot is about ascension.

He smiled at me and said,
"It is the same with our search
For enlightened self and society.
But there are other ways to
View narrative. For example,
While we embrace stories
Where hardship and confusion
Are ultimately overcome by
Compassion and community,
Like in the romance or comedy,
It is also true that a story
Might sing hope and courage
In one scene and then switch
To desire, fear, and ignorance
Just as easily in the next:
This is the tangle of tragedy.
Two masks sit before us,
And every moment is an audition
For the character we will play."

Don't Forget Sutra

Tonight, I was showing the Buddha
My lesson plan for tomorrow's class
When I would introduce my students
To the three essentials of meditation:
The body, the mind, and the breath.

He said, "Don't forget to tell them
That meditation is not an end in itself.
It is a practice in preparing ourselves
For that moment when we will be
Called upon to be calm, attentive,
And clear about what our courage
And compassion are needed for next."

Roller Coaster Sutra

On this beautiful late spring morning,
After breakfast and walking the dog,
I was having tea with the Buddha.
I told him how I was still receiving
Many benefits from my recent retreat.

I said, "One of the most memorable
Teachings was on the causes of misery:
Aversion, craving, and ignorance."
I told him, "I am using these three
Motivations of suffering to interrogate
Almost every situation where I recognize
My own confusion or heightened conflict.
I find great comfort and satisfaction
In the clarity of understanding they provide."

And the Buddha smiled, saying, "I know
That these causes in the abstract may be
Hard to grasp because of their simplicity
and without direct application to experience.
But I do find it helpful to visualize them
In such a way that I can very quickly
Bring them into consciousness.
For example, picture a roller coaster.
This roller coaster is a large continuous loop
Standing in the middle of a carnival.
Going up and over, around and around,
Races a single roller coaster car.
Inside sit craving and aversion.
Craving is very excited with arms
Waving above its head, eyes and mouth
Are wide open, screaming for more.
Aversion or fear is sitting next to craving,

Crouching down as far as possible
Into the back of the roller coaster seat,
Eyes and mouth are clenched tight,
Hands are holding on for dear life;
Fear can't wait for the ride to be over.

On the ground below the roller coaster,
We see the speed control mechanism.
It has two settings: Stop and Fast.
The operator, who represents ignorance,
Has fallen asleep at the switch, eyes shut,
Mouth agape, and the speed is set at Fast.
These three figures represent the causes of misery.
They are trapped in the cycle of *samsara*."

I said, "Yes, I can see that. It's very helpful."

The Buddha added, "One of the benefits
Of these figures, these visualizations,
Is that they help us become more aware of
How we contribute to our own difficulties,
And then how we might locate their opposites.
In my case, I find it helpful to raise courage
In response to fear, calm satisfaction or
Contentment in response to racing desire.
But ignorance, hmm, as you very well know,
That is a constant challenge for all of us.
The good news, though, is that we do know
How to respond to an undisciplined mind
Consumed by aversion and appetite.
All it requires is our body and mind
(Which we just happened to have with us
Everywhere we go, every minute of the day).
Meditation is the mental practice
Available to all who desire to learn

The causes of suffering, providing us
With the focus, calm, and determination
To reduce confusion and conflict at last.
Insight, wisdom, knowledge, understanding,
These are the opposites of ignorance
And lead us to the liberation we all seek.
Look now at craving sitting in contentment,
Fear transformed by courage and kindness,
And the darkness of our ignorance replaced
By this brilliant sunlight we are now enjoying
On this lovely morning with our tea."

Eden Sutra

For the most part, I have escaped
The arthritis that sometimes swells
My hand and wrist as I write or draw,
And I asked the Buddha his view
On the tension between the mind
That seeks new territory and the body
That stumbles on its path as we age.

He smiled at me like the morning sun,
"Unlike many of our friends in nature,
We have evolved in our ability
To escape seasonal life and death.
Yet this advancement has only led us
To new degrees of dissatisfaction.
The farther from the annual turn
We wander, the more we believe
In our immortality, and as a result,
We feel entitled to permanent
Youthfulness, joy, and freedom.
Whether we have risen above nature
Or fallen from it, many have agreed
That our suffering results from this."

Triple Consciousness Sutra

Again, I pressed the Buddha
To help me better understand
My struggle to keep the past
And future from impinging on
My desire to focus on the present.
"Good!" he said. "At least,
You're conscious of your troubles.
It's the first page of your new story.

"Listen, every one of us has been
Asleep for most of our lives,
And so we haven't been aware
Of all that has shaped us.
These powerful influences
Contribute to our happiness,
Our ignorance and suffering,
Our knowledge and courage.

"It's very natural for children
To be unaware of influences:
Their parents and teachers,
The stories they hear,
Their skin and country,
Freedoms inherited,
Oppressions unearned,
Food they shared or missed.

"But we are no longer children,
So we must use our attention
To listen carefully, not only
To our present experience
(Which is difficult enough)
But also to our childhoods,

"And how both are likely writing
  The story we'll hear next."

Enlightened Society Sutra

Saturday morning, I drove over to
The Farmers Market near downtown
To see if the peaches had come in,
And I saw the Buddha had a booth
Set up near the used book tent.
A few people were standing around,
And I heard a young woman ask,
"Can enlightened society really exist?"

He said, "Let's say enlightenment
Is our individual state of joy
And gratitude and respect felt
For our lives and our relationships
With others and the natural world,
A complete embrace of experience,
With a mind continually energized
By new knowledge and glad to
Share it in ways that will benefit
Each other and our planet,
With a heart ready and humble,
Brave in its acceptance of its duty
To empty itself into another's cup
No matter how small and cracked,
And with a body grounded by breath,
Always muscled in its preparation
To hold itself and others high
Above the riptide of suffering.
Now imagine two people who
Not only experience that joy,
That same gratitude and respect,
But recognize it in each other
With such power and surprise
That they dedicate themselves

"To each other's continued joy,
  Gratitude and everlasting respect.

"Now imagine that you are today
  Walking around a market like this,
  And everyone you meet is ready
  To lift you above your riptide;
  You see it in them and they in you.
  It can't happen until it's imagined.
  Belief is the fuel ready to be lit."

Crepe Myrtle Sutra

On Sunday, I met the Buddha
At my favorite breakfast place.
I ordered the sausage scrambler
With whole wheat and mixed fruit.

He said, "I'll just have black coffee."

The music coming over the speakers
Was pretty loud so we sat outside
Under the umbrellas on the patio.
I was telling him about my father,
Locked up in dementia and dying.

The Buddha looked out at the avenue,
Car after car raced to church or golf.
He said, "Look how the crepe myrtles
Today lift their flowers ever so high."

Start Again Sutra

After dinner and dishes, the Buddha and I
Sat outside on the patio, and I described how
Every morning during the meditation retreat,
I would take a short walk before breakfast
Along a narrow path in a small wooded area
From my dormitory to a large open pasture
Where cows grazed and buzzards soared.

"I guess I was the first to walk there each day,"
I told him, "because I kept running into
Spider webs invisibly strung across the path.
Again and again, I wiped them from my face."

"I hope," the Buddha said, "you appreciated
The lesson these little difficulties offered you.
Each morning, we start again in meditation
With small distractions that slow our practice,
But with diligence and patience, we open
A clear path that eventually leads us
To the benefits of owning our own minds."

VII: Encourage

Art Sutra

After the Buddha
Concluded his talk,
He stepped back
From the podium,
And the department
Chair came forward
To start the question
And answer portion
Of the evening.
And the first person
Standing in the aisle
Was a large man
Who had to hunch
Over slightly to speak
Into the microphone.

"I'm very curious
About what you just
Said about the role
Art plays in society.
I think you said
It is a spiritual path
That leads us to
Self-understanding
And to compassion
For others as well.
But what do you say
To those like me
Who don't think they
Are creative at all?"

The Buddha smiled,
Bowed to the man,

And answered slowly,
"Once you understand
There are an infinite
Number of imaginations
Possible, you will see
You have one, too."

Assessment Sutra

I was hunched over my keyboard
Entering the assessment data
For the current academic year:
Benchmarks, measures, rubrics,
And course average results when
The Buddha called to see if we were
Still going to meet for our regular
Afternoon walk around campus.
I said I would leave off entering
The use of results until I returned.

He said, "I am curious about how
You measure the wakefulness
Between students and their studies
And teachers and their teaching.
How do numbers capture that?"

Flying Sutra

I emailed the Buddha after dinner tonight
To tell him about the English teachers
Who were visiting from China and Vietnam,

And how I gave them a poetry lesson today,
And how one of the students after class
Asked me to read his poem, and in the poem

He told how excited he was at first to fly
Away from home, but now after two weeks,
He was ready to fly home and have dreams

In his own bed again, and then I asked him
If he ever had any dreams in which he flew,
And he said, "Yes, very high," but he also said

That he never crashes but always wakes up
Just in time, and another teacher said,
"Yes, me too, but I also never ever crash,"

And then another said, "Yes, it is the same
For me as well," and I said, "In my dreams
I also fly, but it is only above the ground

A few feet, and it's more like swimming
Than flying, and I am showing others
How to do it, saying, it's really very easy,"

And the Buddha replied, "Teaching and
Writing and flying are all fine examples
Of valuable training in the freedom arts."

Battle Sutra

The anger was rising again.

After the retreat, I thought
I'd be able to recognize
And prevent my habit of
Lifting my ego high above
My head, and out of reach
Of my breath and mind,
And this same old heart,
Wanting, so wanting
To be brave in loving:
Even what roars and runs
Right at me without warning.

I remember the Buddha
Taking my hand and saying,
"The battle we fight,
 With nothing more than
 Our mutual brokenness,
 Has never resulted in peace.

"How could we ever think
 To repair pain with pain?

"The only way to engage
 Our anger is to counter it
 With a mind practiced in
 The deep act of awareness,
 Fully steeped in accepting
 The reality of our aggression,
 Requiring our constant
 Vigilance and forgiveness.

"Otherwise, we only breastfeed
Our misery.

   "Hear him cry,
Like a window shattering glass,
A mouthful of pain and darkness.

"Why would we choose to break more glass?"

Good Dog Sutra

I was talking to the Buddha about
When the self must have first learned
That to serve others also serves the self.
I wasn't exactly sure what I meant,
And I think he knew it, too, but he said,

"Selflessness cannot really be selfless
 If the self wants to get better at it.
 Do you think your good dog who
 Works outside all day and protects
 You inside at night is selfless in his
 Service to you so he can eat well?
 Your neighborhood is only safe
 If your neighbors want your safety, too."

Begin Again Sutra

As I was meditating hard
To achieve my authenticity,
I was startled by the Buddha
Who walked in uninvited
And flopped himself down
On the couch of my mind.

"This is no way to proceed,"
He said. "What you are after
Is a permanent and stable
Version of yourself you can
Unfold and display at will,
When all along you ignore
The self who wishes to be
Anyone but the self he is.
Begin again with forgiveness
For the one you already are
And the generosity you need
To help others see the same."

Bluebonnet Sutra

This weekend, the Buddha and I drove
To the Hill Country to see the bluebonnets,
And on the return trip home I asked him
About how he was able to overcome
The suffering so many of us continue to
Wrestle with in our lives, and he rolled up
His window so he could be better heard
Saying,

      "Our suffering is to a large degree
The result of the fear we feel about being
Ourselves. In other words, much of our
Common suffering is a self-imposed
Despair that we unknowingly practice
In hope that our friends and family
Will rush to our rescue, when in truth,
The only ones who can come to our aid
Is a patient heart and a ready mind."

Decision Sutra

The Buddha came by for Sunday brunch,
And I was telling him how I've begun
To accept just how easily distracted I am.
And looking up from his bowl, he said,

"You are not alone in these difficulties.
When we're distracted by the past,
We can't see what's right in front of us,
And when we're distracted by the future,
We can't hear what the past is trying to tell us.
But the past and future aren't only distractions,
They also represent a series of single moments
When decisions were made or likely will be.
Making good decisions in these moments
Not only requires a good amount of practice,
But also an open heart, a disciplined mind,
And strong trust in our ability to envision
What will serve ourselves and others best.
Meditation offers us this kind of practice
In moment to moment decision-making
By focusing our body, breath, and mind
On the best choices we have available to us,
Like how you made this delicious oatmeal
By adding just the right amount of raisins."

Whittling Sutra

Every weekend, when my wife and I clean house,
And before I release the vacuuming beast,
I move around my books and magazines to dust.
I have subscribed to and Amazoned more than
I'll ever get to, especially my growing library
Of volumes on meditation and Buddhism.
I told the Buddha how it was high time to whittle down.

"The popularity of these authors and topics
 Amazes even me," he said. "But we mustn't let
 The noise silence the silence. The basics remain
 The same. Stop. Breathe. Listen. Encourage."

VIII: Into Flight

Chorus Sutra

After the evening concert,
I told the Buddha how much
I was inspired by the choir's
Performance and how unified
In purpose they seemed,
"I wish everyone I knew
 Might find such harmony."

He paused on the sidewalk
And smiled at me saying,
"From birth we are taught
 Habits that strengthen
 And unify consciousness
 By constantly pairing
Our mind and our body
In a common purpose.
But there are also teachers
Who want us to keep these
Good friends at a distance.
The mind drifts away.
The body is lost in the street.
How can we expect
To join together as one
When we are divided
Even against ourselves?
Self-knowledge is the path
To enlightened society,
But harmony can only be
Built upon the beauty
And love we find and
Sing with on the road."

Otherwise Sutra

I was having lunch
With the Buddha
And explained how
I was rethinking ways
I might teach my classes
In the coming year.
I said, "I need reminding
That the central aim
Of all of my teaching
Is to help students
See the permanent value
Of the simple practices
I am asking them to use
To learn about themselves,
Others, and the world."

The Buddha smiled
And replied slowly,
"Staying focused on
 The simple truths
 Is always difficult.
 Our suffering comes
 From practices
 That ignore
 Our impermanence.
 But if we understand
 That our suffering
 Is already included
 In all that's impermanent,
 We can ignore
 Those practices
 And choose otherwise."

Earth Protector Sutra

Sad news today about the Sakyong.

In my office at school, I am looking
Over my bookshelf and the volumes
I've read by Mipham and his father,
Many I've assigned to my students.

Why am I surprised at this inflamed
Appetite and body craving that always
Shadows the shining of celebrity power
And rising entitlement of male desire?

The Buddha knocks on my door
And asks if we might discuss this lesson.
But I have to leave to teach a class,
So we walk up the stairway together.

The steps seem very steep.

Species Sutra

The Buddha emailed me a link
To a recent article on progress
In human genome modification
And the worry some have about
Creating a super human species
Potentially smarter and stronger
Than anyone we might imagine,
Adding,

      "It's curious to me why
Such discussions in technology
Focus on genetic improvements
Benefitting the mind and the body
But never on the need to increase
Our chances for enlightenment
And compassion for one another.
This new science may be useful,
But it will never help us remove
The suffering from our hearts."

Presence Sutra

I was looking through a new app
Offering guided meditations,
Online classes, and relaxing music
To accompany my morning practice,
And it occurred to me to ask
The Buddha when he decided
Being present was the one true
Antidote to universal suffering.
He nodded, smiled, and said,

"As I began to work with my mind
 To sort out the distractions of
 Fear, craving, and ignorance
 From the truths of impermanence,
 Courage, compassion, and contentment,
 I realized the only time I was able
 To achieve this work was in the present
 At the leading edge of every instant,
 Again and again, breath after breath.
 Right now is the only moment we have
 To decide what to allow into our minds
 Or what to reject over and over again.
 We have so much important work to do:
 We must set intentions and always
 Keep a vigilant eye on the path.
 We have to consider how our actions
 Will benefit those we care about.
 We have to pay close attention to
 The constant threat of our selfishness.
 With all of these challenges before us,
 I concluded we have two options:
 We can vacate our humanity
 And enslave our minds to others,

"Or we can pay attention to our decisions
At every step, always ready to remove
The causes of our misery, claiming
Each remaining moment for good."

Focus Sutra

About midway through our road trip,
I was filling up the car
As the Buddha went into the restroom
And paid for the gas.
And once we were on the road again,
I resumed my complaint
About the problem of mindfulness
And the constant nagging
Of the past and future upon my life,
And I reviewed my difficulties
In creating any kind of sustained focus
Or span of attention
That might create the transformative
Light of contentment
I was seeking from my daily practice.
And from behind the wheel,
The Buddha turned to me and said,

"The point is to make more time,
 Not lose it worrying about perfecting
 Your training in consciousness.
 The only place where more time can be
 Made is here in the present
 By attending to who you are
 So that you can better attend to others."
 Adding, "I thought you said
 You were going to clean the windshield."

Postgame Sutra

I finished my early morning meditation
With my wife and dogs, calmly listening
To an online teaching on how to achieve
A relaxed awareness of the sensations
Of the breath and body, and expanding
Outward to the awareness of the sounds
Emanating from the world around us,
And then closing with a guided return
To the body and breath, followed by
A soft bell at the end of the session.

Afterward, as my wife began her shower,
I found the Buddha standing in the kitchen.
"How was your practice this morning?"
He asked. "Are these recorded sessions
Helpful in attaining a beneficial mind?"

"Yes," I said. "I think they are useful,
Though they often follow the same path
Of settling in with a focus on the breath,
Then guiding the attention outward,
And finally returning to the breath again.
Still, I find it curious that they fail
To acknowledge that period right after
The bell at the close of the session.
By that I mean, they don't account for
The time we need to pause and remember
What we might have achieved in sitting,
To reflect upon an insight we acquired,
A postgame review of lessons learned."

"I think I know what you mean," he said,
"Kind of like what you're doing right now."

Wings Sutra

On this hot Sunday, I told the Buddha about
Our morning walk around the neighborhood.

Marie-Clare and I saw a Cooper's Hawk perched
High on a bare branch of a withering pecan.

We paused to point, and suddenly he dropped,
Swooping in a slow circle around us.

As he swung back up to his top spot,
I said, "I think we just received his blessing."

Higher up in the blue, a batch of buzzards circled,
Rising on a column of simmering air.

"What a feeling that must be," I said,
"To soar so effortlessly, without a care."

"Oh, you bet there's effort," said the Buddha.
"It's not that easy to turn stillness into flight."

IX: Listen Again

Dignity Sutra

I told the Buddha about the insight
I had this morning in meditation.
As my wife and I sat in our bedroom,
A new soft rain drifted down south
Out of Abilene and Big Spring,
Coughing thunder above a crisp August.

Over the tiny speaker of my phone,
Our meditation guide told us to sit
In dignity as we counted our breath.
I said, "I realized then the intention
Of meditation was not to reach for
The unattainable perfect attention,
But to forgive the wandering mind.

"It's only in that acceptance, yes?
That we practice the habit we need
Of reminding the mind in kindness
To return to the pool of presence
Always patient for our awareness.
Without distraction, we will never
Notice we've left the path we desire,
Never start again in dignity."

Scribe Sutra

When I presented to the Buddha
The transcripts of his teachings
I had been assigned to record,
He asked me to walk with him
And to read what I had written.

Slowly, I climbed inside the words
I had heard and remembered,
Looking upon him often for
Some light of approval in his eyes.
But nothing was revealed.

In the darkness of the forest,
I thought I heard his tall voice echo,
Calling out for a better tongue
Than the one I was able to pull
From my rough inked pages.

He said, "It's one thing to listen.
Another to write what you've heard.
Yet another to read what you've written.
Still another to hear what you are reading.
The only lesson left is to listen again."